Bear Photo Album

©1990 Dee and Tom Hockenberry
All rights reserved. No part of this book may be reproduced or utilized in any form or by any means, electronic or mechanical, including photocopying, recording, or by an information storage and retrieval system, without the permission in writing from the publisher. Inquiries should be addressed to Hobby House Press, Inc., 900 Frederick Street, Cumberland, Maryland 21502.

Printed in the United States of America

ISBN: 087588-358-3

Published by Hobby House Press

Cumberland, Maryland 21502

Dee & Tom Hockenberry

Dedicated to our families

Acknowledgements

To Gary, Carolyn, Dave, Donna, and all the staff at Hobby House Press for their faith and friendship which makes our association such a pleasure. To the Hurd family for allowing us to photograph at their beautiful market. To Lorraine for everything.
Thank you all.

TABLE OF CONTENTS

Introduction 2
Winter 3
Spring 19
Summer 43
Fall 65
Christmas 89

Introduction

This is my world and I welcome you to it. I am, as you can see, a rather large bear of impeccable lineage. I am also, I hasten to add, a genial fellow given to simple pleasures and quite humble in spite of auspicious beginnings. I live in a den in a rural community peopled with teddies of all ages, sizes and heritage. There are also various animals who are in residence periodically. The uninitiated might consider them toys but let me tell you, we bears know better.

The animals that everyone considers real are two humans and one cat. The humans are fun to live with and always greet a new arrival with excitement. There always seems to be enough room in heart and hearth for one more. The cat is named Adolf (benefit of a little mustache) but everyone calls him Puddy. He just turned up at the door one snowy winter and liked us so well, he decided to stay.

Our house is situated on the edge of a woods with a creek meandering through the property. Every season is full blown so we can enjoy all nature has to offer. Our woods provide a wildlife sanctuary; thus, our garden abounds with birds, rabbits and chipmunks. A fat woodchuck pays a daily visit and the occasional deer wanders up the path. Once we even saw wild turkey and most surprising of all were two salmon who swam all the way up the creek from the lake.

Our pleasures and pastimes are simple and homespun but then teddies are not very sophisticated anyway. Each day offers new delights and adventures as you will see. Let us open the door; the teddies will be so happy to see you and we invite you to enter our kingdom. Please stay awhile and become a part of our world.

The winter season for us officially begins at New Years. We can expect a bountiful supply of snow and at times are even snowbound. The trees are stripped of their leaves but some apples still cling to the orchard trees and attract the deer from deep in the woods. The world around us turns to silver and white and out come the skates, sleds and warm mufflers. Inside the blazing fireplace keeps us cozy and warm. A new year has begun.

Winter

On New Year's Eve the lines waiting to use the bathrooms are formidable. Some of us are quite venerable and looking our best tends to take more time with each passing year. We all agree that for the biggest party of the year we must look beautiful.

Trying to decide between jet beads and pearls is a problem. Hurry with the makeup; others are waiting to get in. Steiff teddy bear: 16in (41cm), circa 1907. Steiff teddy bear: 20in (51cm), circa 1904.

The faucet angle allows us to shower in the sink. Brushing keeps our coat clean and shiny. Steiff *Dickie* replica teddy bear: 12in (31cm), circa 1985. Schuco yes/no teddy bear: 12in (31cm), circa 1950.

4

The frozen stream has broken up a bit and the visiting seal enjoys a swim and rock to catch a bit of sun for drying off. Brrr — too cold for us teddies. Steiff seal: 6in (15cm), circa 1955.

We toast a new beginning with just a sip, for we already are full of "spirit." Noisemakers and hats add to our gaiety and the twins portray "Father Time" and the "New Baby." Steiff teddy bear: 18in (46cm), circa 1910. Steiff teddy bear: 20in (51cm), circa 1907. Steiff teddy bear: 20 in (51cm), circa 1904. Schuco yes/no teddy bears: 13in (33cm), circa 1925.

Ice fishing is more to our taste and what a catch! Steiff teddy bear: 20in (51cm), circa 1904. Steiff wooden fish on line, circa 1970.

When the wind is howling outside and a case of the sniffles seems imminent, there is nothing cozier than snuggling amidst pillows on the chaise longue. Oh such bliss! I seem to have everything — an afghan, my glasses and best of all, a good magazine to read. Steiff teddy bear: 29in (74cm), circa 1910.

Puddy loves teddies, too. Steiff teddy bear: 12in (31cm), circa 1910. Hockenberry cat: 17in (43cm), circa 1980.

Twirling on the ice...shades of Katarina Witt! Schuco yes/no teddy bear: 12½in (31cm), circa 1950.

Ready for take off. All systems go! Steiff teddy bears: 24in (60cm) and 20in (51cm), circa 1955.

What a fabulous snowman. Aren't we clever? Steiff tail moves head teddy bear: 7in (18cm), circa 1950. Steiff teddy bear: 9in (23cm), 1912.

Toasting by the fire. Steiff teddy bear: 29in (74cm), circa 1910. Steiff teddy bear: 20in (51cm), 1907.

The great profile. Steiff teddy bear: 20in (51cm), circa 1907.

Puddy joins us as we read by the window. He just loves stories about mice. Steiff teddy bear: 24in (60cm), circa 1904. Steiff teddy bear: 20in (51cm), circa 1904.

18

The last trace of snow disappears. Our muddy paw prints, a by-product of spring rains, accelerate the need for a flurry of housecleaning and we are all kept busy. The barren trees seem almost bleak without their coating of white. But look! Almost overnight the world is green, tulips sway in the gentle breeze and the azaleas burst forth in a riot of color. It is time to plan and do all the things we have only dreamed of during the long winter.

Spring

The March wind doth blow and kites flying in the wind turn all eyes upward. First, of course, *Zotty* has to figure how to get it together. Steiff teddy bear *Zotty*: 20in (51cm), circa 1950. Steiff *Roloplan* kite, circa 1950.

In fact, sometimes I feel so dreamy, the world seems hazy and unreal. Steiff teddy bear: 29in (74cm), circa 1910.

One of the first orders of spring is planting geraniums in the large tub. Schuco yes/no musical teddy bear: 20in (51cm), circa 1948. Steiff teddy bear: 20in (51cm), circa 1904.

Spirits run high at the first breath of warm air. *Bully Dog* let his outside freedom overpower him and *Griz* was forced to seek sanctuary up a tree. *Griz* teddy bear: 18in (46cm), handmade bear from commercial pattern, 1980. Steiff *Bully Dog,* circa 1910.

24

The sun shines brightly and it is time to lead the young colt out of the barn. This bear imagines himself a cowboy. Steiff teddy bear: 12in (31cm), circa 1910. Steiff colt, circa 1948.

A ride through the woods in the dapple green of newly leafed trees is a splendid experience. English teddy bear by Casa Roma: 23in (58cm), 1983. Horse on wheels: German, circa 1910.

The little stone bear is brought out of hibernation to decorate the terrace. Schuco yes/no teddy bear: 12in (31cm), 1953.

Teddy eyes the beehive the stone bear is clutching and is reminded of the one high up in a tree. Stick in hand, he makes his perilous journey to partake of a drop or two of honey. Steiff teddy bear: 15in (38cm), 1903.

This large rock is right in our front yard and all manner of bears play upon it. Did you ever see these two together before? Steiff honey and polar bears: 4in (10cm), circa 1950.

Velvety pansies are one of the first spring delights. Koala has taken time to smell the flowers. Steiff koala: 5in (13cm), circa 1955.

Getting marshmallows from the cupboard is an Olympian task. A veritable relay effort is necessary but that is what team spirit is all about. Schuco yes/no teddy bear: 13in (33cm), circa 1925. Hermann teddy bear: 9in (23cm), circa 1950. Steiff teddy bear: 12in (31cm), circa 1910.

A circle of stones is a safety precaution in containing our small fire. The marshmallows are so delicious and the shadows and sounds of the woods add to our pleasure. Steiff teddy bear: 13½in (34cm), circa 1950. Steiff teddy bear: 12in (31cm), circa 1910. Steiff teddy bear: 11in (28cm), circa 1908.

A rainy day calls for the ritual of afternoon tea. It is a time to discuss what inside activities would be the most fun. Schuco yes/no teddy bear: 22in (56cm), circa 1925. Steiff teddy bear: 20in (51cm), circa 1904.

"A play" they shouted in unison. Up to the box room they scrambled to go through the cartons and drawers to try and unearth some suitable costumes. There is nothing quite like the comforting sound of raindrops on the roof. It is a nostalgic atmosphere and so the teddies spend the afternoon exclaiming over treasures and thinking their own private thoughts. Steiff teddy bear: 18in (46cm), circa 1910. Steiff teddy bear: 12in (31cm), circa 1935. Steiff clown teddy bear: 13in (33cm), circa 1929. Schuco yes/no teddy bear: 5in (13cm), circa 1955.

A play, thought teddy, is a fine form of entertainment, but the opera! Now that is thrilling! I could sing "Pagliacci," he mused, while the audience sits enthralled. Schuco yes/no teddy bear: 5in (13cm), circa 1955.

The sun shines again, as always and glistens on *Zotty's* luxurious coat as he sits upon riding bear in the window to enjoy to warmth. Steiff *Zotty* teddy bear: 14½in (37cm), circa 1960. Steiff riding bear on wheels, circa 1910.

Once upon a time a big red dog lived with us. He left us for a place in the sky but we will always remember his beautiful face. We content ourselves with hugging *Bully* now who thinks he is beautiful, too, and suffers our bouts of affection. Gund sailor Bialosky teddy bear: 18in (46cm), 1982. Steiff *Bully Dog* on wheels, circa 1930.

A backpacking trip through the woods is as pleasant in the spring as in the fall. How exciting it is to come upon the deer wandering up the path. Gund backpack Bialosky teddy bear: 18in (46cm), 1985. Steiff deer on wheels, circa 1910.

Easter Sunday is the day to don our finery and prepare to lift our voices in song and worship. Steiff teddy bear: 24in (60cm), circa 1904. Schuco yes/no teddy bear: 22in (56cm), circa 1925. Steiff teddy bear: 20in (51cm), circa 1907. Steiff teddy bear: 19in (48cm), circa 1950.

42

The sounds and sights of summer are upon us. Feel the summer air. Sometimes it lies on one's cheek like a soft caress and in the dog days, it is heavy and moist. It is a time for lemonade and reading on the porch, for vacations or just watching the roses unfold. The sound of school buses is replaced by the sound of tractors in nearby fields. The songbirds' melodies echo through the woods and squirrels chatter all day long. Our pace is slower and in some ways it is the nicest season of all.

Summer

On a lazy summer day there is nothing finer than donning a straw hat and lowering our pail into the stream. Sometimes we are lucky. Will you look at the fish! Steiff teddy bear: 16in (41cm), circa 1910. Steiff *Flossie* fish, circa 1955.

The pandas are considered bears now and show their delight at becoming bona fide family members. Steiff panda: 10in (25cm), circa 1950. Steiff panda: 6in (15cm), circa 1950.

Yikes! *Muffet* did not expect a guest as she tried to enjoy her bowl of whey. Steiff teddy bear: 16in (41cm), circa 1905. Steiff *Spidy,* circa 1958.

The fields of golden grain are ready to be harvested. Schuco yes/no musical teddy bear: 20in (51cm), circa 1948.

The harrow sits idle in mid summer waiting for another season to be put to use. It is fun to climb and play upon. Steiff teddy bear: 20in (51cm), circa 1904.

The English lead garden rabbit amidst the summer blooms beckons teddy to become a part of the beautiful pageant. Steiff teddy bear: 15in (38cm), 1903.

49

After a summer shower, all manner of fungi spring up on the lawn. *Nelly* snail finds a toadstool the perfect vantage point. Steiff *Nelly* snail, circa 1955.

Surprised to see such a large mushroom at the edge of the orchard, the sprite-like teddy hurried over and was amazed to see a woods elf. Schuco yes/no teddy bear: 22in (56cm), circa 1925. Schuco yes/no dwarf, circa 1925.

Sitting alone on the bank of the stream is restful. It is the perfect spot to dream and contemplate. Steiff teddy bear: 16in (41cm), circa 1905.

Kneehigh by the Fourth of July. Hermann teddy bear: 20in (51cm), circa 1955.

This year we decided on a windjammer cruise for our vacation. The bellhop bear always helps to pack....suitcases seem to be his lot in life. Do not forget warm sweaters and especially the telescope for we might spot a whale. Schuco yes/no *Teddy Messenger*: 11in (28cm), circa 1925. Steiff *Zotty* teddy bear: 14½in (37cm), circa 1960.

We are glad we traveled to the coast for lobster is delicious. Steiff teddy bear: 16in (41cm), circa 1908. Steiff lobster, circa 1960.

All ready and prepared to be a seaman in his sailor suit, teddy meets the captain of our ship on the waterway pier. Schuco yes/no teddy bear: 12in (31cm), circa 1950. Steiff doll: circa 1913.

Down the channel we sail on the way to the big ocean. What exhilaration we feel to at last be on our way. Schuco perfume teddy bear: 5in (13cm), circa 1925. Steiff teddy bear: 3½in (9cm), circa 1950.

Home again, Puppy follows eagerly for he knows there are not only cookies in the basket, but doggy biscuits as well. Steiff musical teddy bear: 13½in (34cm), circa 1950. Steiff *Theophil* dog: circa 1970.

We are surfeited with fried chicken and deviled eggs (the traditional picnic fare) and now we rest under the leafy trees just nibbling occasionally on fruit and honey (our traditional picnic fare). Steiff teddy bear: 11½in (29cm), circa 1907. Steiff teddy bear: 16in (41cm), circa 1957. Steiff google-eyed *Petsy* teddy bear: 9in (23cm), circa 1958. Steiff teddy bear: 11in (28cm), circa 1935.

Picking plump, juicy berries results in the jams and jellies we will feast upon all year long. Schuco yes/no teddy bear: 17in (43cm), circa 1925.

Joe cool himself! The air is warm and still and floating on the pond is so refreshing. Teddies cannot swim, you know. Canterbury teddy bear: 15in (38cm), 1983.

Across the pond two rowers cause barely a ripple in the water. Steiff teddy bears: 3½in (9cm), circa 1950.

Once a year we celebrate everyone's birthday, since none of the teddies recall their exact date. We picked the summer season so we could have our cake and balloons at the glass table on the terrace. The traditional "crackers" provide paper hats and tiny treasures. Steiff teddy bear: 20in (51cm), circa 1904. Steiff teddy bear: 24in (60cm), circa 1904. Steiff teddy bear: 18in (46cm), circa 1910.

One of our favorite things. Steiff teddy bear: 12in (31cm), circa 1935.

62

Wild flowers can often be as lovely as those cultivated. Witness "Queen Anne" admiring her lace. Steiff teddy bear: 16in (41cm), circa 1910.

The first day of school is exciting and scary. Our books are ready and, of course, an apple for the teacher. Artist teddy bear designed and executed by author: 18in (46cm), 1982. Schuco yes/no teddy bear: 13in (33cm), circa 1948.

Fall

The autumn season bursts forth in a display of crimson, bronze, orange and yellow. The sky is alive with Canadian geese heading south. Sometimes there is a nip in the air and at other times the sun shines with a warmth so tender that even sweaters are not needed. Outside activity abounds for we feel a need to do all the things not possible when winter comes. There is work to do, as well, in preparation for cold weather. We revel in the merriment of trick or treating at Halloween and give thanks for our blessings (and turkey!) as Thanksgiving Day is celebrated.

Goodbye. Hurry home. Maybe next year we can go to school, too. In the meantime perhaps the scholars can teach us a thing or two. Steiff teddy bears: 13in (33cm), circa 1950. Handmade teddy bear: 14in (36cm), 1983. Steiff teddy bear: 13in (33cm), circa 1950.

Sitting at the old desk is a learning experience. The scroll has all manner of information and we copy letters on the blackboard top. Steiff teddy bear: 24in (60cm), circa 1904. Steiff *Minky Zotty* teddy bear: 10in (25cm), circa 1960. Steiff *Zolac* teddy bear: 14in (36cm), circa 1964.

Let us root for a member of the home team as he practices for a big game. North American bear *Kareem Abdul Jabear*: 24in (60cm), 1986.

Taking photographs is a great hobby and the fall foliage provides an interesting background. Schuco yes/no musical teddy bear: 16in (41cm), circa 1950. Steiff *Zotty* teddy bear: 14½in (37cm), circa 1960.

This picture came out just grand. American teddy bear — possibly Ideal: 22in (56cm), circa 1910.

It is hard to sit still but it was managed. English teddy bear: 21½in (55cm), circa 1925.

The berries on the hawthorn tree attract all manner of birds. Steiff finch *Gimpel*: 4in (10cm), circa 1955.

The falling leaves cover the ground like a blanket. Raking them is a task for some of us and playtime for others. Steiff teddy bear: 29in (74cm), circa 1910. Schuco yes/no teddy bear: 13in (33cm), circa 1925. Steiff teddy bear: 16in (41cm), circa 1910.

A closer look at that beautiful bird necessitates a little tree climbing. Chinese teddy bear: 17in (43cm), circa 1982.

73

Help! Schuco yes/no teddy bear: 13in (33cm), circa 1925.

Nature's wonder. All these colors from the same maple tree. Steiff teddy bear: 3½in (9cm), circa 1950.

Mr. Badger has come out of his lair to gather apples for his winter store. Teddy watches and hopes he does not frighten him. Steiff teddy bear: 18in (46cm), circa 1950. Steiff studio badger: 25in (64cm), circa 1960.

When the temperature dips on a brisk fall day, we are reminded that a supply of wood will be needed for the long winter ahead. Steiff teddy bear: 29in (74cm), circa 1910. Steiff cozy teddy bear: 11in (28cm), circa 1955.

A rest after yardwork or play is the order of the day. English teddy bear: 36in (91cm), circa 1930.

During a walk in the woods the teddies not only come upon a strangely growing tree, but also a fox! Steiff teddy bear: 16in (41cm), circa 1910. Steiff teddy bear: 14in (36cm), circa 1950. Schuco yes/no teddy bear: 17in (43cm), circa 1925.

The fox sits up at attention, as surprised to see us as we are at seeing him. Steiff studio fox: 21½in (55cm), circa 1955.

When the fox ran away we huddled on the uprooted tree roots. Of course, we were not really scared! Steiff teddy bear: 16in (41cm), circa 1910. Steiff teddy bear: 14in (36cm), circa 1956. Schuco yes/no teddy bear: 17in (43cm), circa 1925.

The goblins will get you if you don't watch out! Steiff teddy bear: 29in (74cm), circa 1910.

A little pumpkin just my size. Steiff teddy bear: 9in (23cm), circa 1912.

The lowly thistle has a form of great beauty. Steiff teddy bear: 12in (31cm), circa 1911.

It is time to sing and dance and welcome in the harvest. Steiff teddy bear: 29in (74cm), circa 1910. Steiff teddy bear: 24in (60cm), circa 1904. Steiff teddy bear: 20in (51cm), circa 1950.

Nature's bounty is in abundance at our favorite market. Our state's famous apples bring visions of pie fresh from the oven and the glorious mums add color to the landscape. Steiff teddy bear: 20in (51cm), circa 1904.

One last tree climbing escapade before the snow and ice prevent it. Steiff teddy bear: 16in (41cm), circa 1910. Steiff teddy bear: 20in (51cm), circa 1907. Schuco yes/no teddy bear: 12in (31cm), circa 1950.

Squash to bake and flowers for the table insure a happy Thanksgiving. Steiff teddy bear: 24in (60cm), circa 1904.

Christmas seems like a fifth season for it begins right after Thanksgiving. The aroma of baking cookies fills the house, presents are bought and wrapped, and forages for long-needled pine branches fill our days. The mantle and bannister are roped with greens and boxes of ornaments strew the house. The first week of December begins the decorating in earnest and when all is ready, we are starry-eyed with wonder. It is a magical time.

Shiny papers and bright ribbons to wrap the surprises. Steiff teddy bear: 29in (74cm), circa 1910. Steiff teddy bear: 18in (46cm), circa 1910. Steiff teddy bears: 13in (33cm), circa 1955.

Christmas

Each ornament is a remembrance of yules gone by. Steiff teddy bears: 12½in (32cm), circa 1957. Steiff teddy bear: 7in (18cm), circa 1950. Steiff teddy bear: 11in (28cm), circa 1912.

Pouring cocoa for the season's party. The chocolate-covered peanut butter wreath is simply delectable. Steiff teddy bear: 18in (46cm), circa 1910. Steiff teddy bear: 12in (31cm), circa 1910.

Sliding down a pine-roped banister is a little hazardous but each year teddy manages it. Steiff teddy bear: 16in (41cm), circa 1907.

Can that be Santa's helper? *Jester* bear and friend designed and executed by author: 18in (46cm) and 6in (15cm), 1986. Steiff riding bear: circa 1910.

The stockings are hung by the chimney with care. Steiff teddy bear: 29in (74cm), 1910.

In hopes that St. Nicholas soon would be there. Schuco yes/no teddy bear: 8in (20cm), 1950.

Not a creature was stirring. Steiff teddy bear: 12in (31cm), circa 1910. Steiff *Pieps* mouse, circa 1955.

The colors and lights of Christmas and may all your days be as merry and bright.

Another year is drawing to a close. We have experienced joys, adventures and contentment. It has been a pleasure to welcome you into our world and remember the door is always open.

Goodbye. Goodbye. Come again!

Finis